NNAT®
GRADE 2
NNAT3 Level C

ABOUT ORIGINS PUBLICATIONS

Origins Publications helps students develop their higher-order thinking skills while also improving their chances of admission into gifted and accelerated learner programs.

Our goal is to unleash and nurture the genius in every student. We do this by offering educational and test prep materials that are fun, challenging and provide a sense of accomplishment.

Please contact us with any questions.
info@originspublications.com

Copyright© 2019 by Origins Publications
Written and Edited by: Gifted and Talented Test Preparation Team

ISBN:978-1-948255-90-5

The Naglieri Nonverbal Ability Test® (NNAT®) is a registered trademark of NCS Pearson Inc., which is not affiliated with Origins Publications. NCS Pearson Inc. has not endorsed the contents of this book.

BONUS

DOWNLOAD YOUR NNAT PRACTICE TEST

IN

COLOR

If you also want the COLOR version of this book, please go to the following link to download it!

Please visit
https://originstutoring.lpages.co/nnat135

to access the color version of the practice test.

Contents

Part 1: Introduction to the NNAT®

This book offers an overview of the types of questions on the Naglieri Nonverbal Ability Test (NNAT) Level C, test-taking strategies to improve performance, and one full-length NNAT® Level C practice test that students can use to assess their knowledge and practice their test-taking skills.

Who Takes the NNAT® Level C?

The NNAT® Level C is often used as an assessment tool or admissions test in 2nd grade for entry into 3rd grade of gifted and talented programs and highly-competitive schools. The NNAT® Level C is also used as an assessment tool by teachers to figure out which students would benefit from an accelerated or remedial curriculum.

When Does the NNAT® Take Place?

This depends on the school district you reside in or want to attend. Check with the relevant school/ district to learn more about test dates and the application/ registration process.

NNAT® Level C Overview

The NNAT® is designed to assess the cognitive skills that relate to academic success in school for students between four and 18. The questions on the NNAT® consist of geometric figures, shapes, and symbols. A child must use visual reasoning and logical thinking to decipher the answers. The test does not require a child to be able to read, write or speak in the English Language.

Length

The NNAT® has 48 multiple-choice questions and offers both an online version and a paper and pencil test. It takes approximately 30 minutes to complete.

Format

The official NNAT® test has only 3 colors: blue, orange and green. (The color green was recently added in the most recent edition of the NNAT). This book is in black and white, but you can download the color version from our website. Get the link from the page at the begining or end of this book.

Part 2: How to Use this Book

The NNAT® is an important test and the more a student is familiar with the questions on the exam, the better she will fare when taking the test.

This book will help your student get used to the format and content of the test so s/he will be adequately prepared and feel confident on test day.

Inside this book, you will find:

- Overview of each question type on the test and teaching tips to help your child approach each question type strategically and with confidence.

- 1 full-length NNAT® Level C practice test and answer keys.

Part 3. Test Prep Tips and Strategies

Firstly, and most importantly, commit to make the test preparation process a stress-free one. A student's ability to keep calm and focused in the face of challenge is a quality that will benefit him or her throughout his or her academic life.

Be prepared for difficult questions from the get-go! There will be a certain percentage of questions that are very challenging for all children. It is key to encourage students to use all strategies available when faced with challenging questions. And remember that a student can get quite a few questions wrong and still do very well on the test.

Before starting the practice test, go through the sample questions and read the general test prep strategies provided at the beginning of the book. They will help you guide your student as he or she progresses through the practice test.

The following strategies may also be useful as you help your child prepare:

Before You Start

- Find a quiet, comfortable spot to work free of distractions.
- Tell your student you will be doing some fun activities.
- Show your student how to perform the simple technique of shading (and erasing) bubbles.

During Prep

- Encourage your student to carefully consider all the answer options before selecting one. Tell him or her there is only ONE answer.
- Encourage your student to visualise the correct answer in the empty box before checking the answer options.
- If your student is stumped by a question, she or he can use the process of elimination. First, encourage your student to eliminate obviously wrong answers to narrow down the answer choices. If your student is still in doubt after using this technique, tell him or her to guess as there are no points deducted for wrong answers.

- If challenged by a question, ask your student to explain why he or she chose a specific answer. If the answer was incorrect, this will help you identify where your student is stumbling. If the answer was correct, asking your student to articulate her reasoning aloud will help reinforce the concept.
- Review all the questions your student answered incorrectly, and explain to your student why the answer is incorrect. Have your student attempt these questions again a few days later to see if he or she now understands the concept.
- Encourage your student to do his or her best, but take plenty of study breaks. Start with 10-15 minute sessions. Your student will perform best if she views these activities as fun and engaging, not as exercises to be avoided.

When to Start Preparing?

Every family and student will approach preparation for this test differently. There is no 'right' way to prepare; there is only the best way for a particular child and family. We suggest students take one full-length practice test and spend 6-8 hours reviewing NNAT® practice questions.

If you have limited time to prepare, spend most energy reviewing areas where your student is encountering the majority of problems.

As they say, knowledge is power! Preparing for the NNAT® will certainly help your student avoid anxiety and make sure she does not give up too soon when faced with unfamiliar and perplexing questions.

Part 4: Question Types and Teaching Tips

The NNAT® Level C is comprised of four different question types:

Pattern Completion
Reasoning by Analogy
Serial Reasoning
Spatial Visualization

Each question type involves the following steps:

- The student is presented with a picture of a matrix.
- The student must observe and detect the relationship among the parts of the matrix.
- The student must solve the problem based on the information shown to her within the matrix, and choose the correct answer from five possible options.

Pattern Completion

With this question type, the student is presented with a design in a rectangle. Inside the large rectangle is a smaller white rectangle representing a missing piece that completes the design. The student must choose the answer that best fits the inner rectangle so that the missing parts complete the design.

These questions are the most common question types found on the Level A and B tests, and they are the easiest kinds of matrices in the exam. On the Level C exam, these question types appear relatively less frequently.

When your students encounters this kind of question for the first few times, say:

"Look at the picture. A piece is missing where you see the question mark. Show me the piece that is missing in the answer choices."

After seeing these questions a few times, your student will probably not need this prompt and will spontaneously point to or mark an answer.

SAMPLE QUESTION:

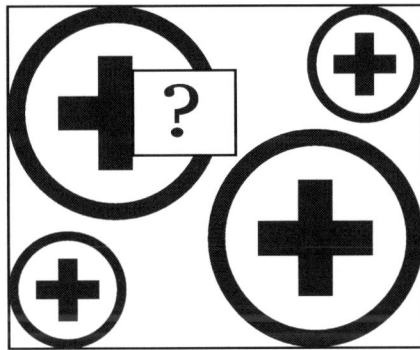

Ⓐ   Ⓑ   Ⓒ   Ⓓ   Ⓔ

Answer: C

TIPS:
Ask your student to complete the picture by continuing the correct lines and colors of the design into the empty box. Then, match the drawing with the correct answer choice.

Ask your student to note the color/shade and design next to the corners of the empty box as this is a useful base to help identify the correct answer.

Go through each answer option and ask the student to visualize how each choice would fit the design.

Reasoning by Analogy

With this question type, the child is presented with a matrix of 4-6 boxes containing objects, usually geometric shapes.

To solve the problem, the child must determine how the object changes as it moves across the row and down the column in the matrix. The question may require that the student pay close attention to several aspects of the design (e.g: shading, color, shape) at the same time.

When your students encounters this kind of question for the first few times, say:

"Look at the picture. A piece is missing where you see the question mark. Show me the piece that is missing in the answer choices."

SAMPLE QUESTION:

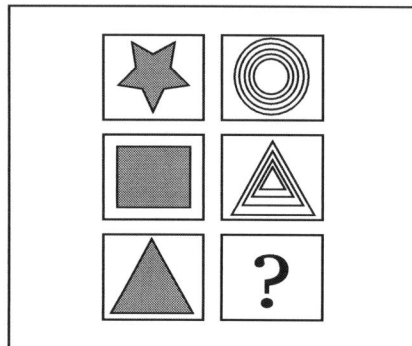

Ⓐ   Ⓑ   Ⓒ   Ⓓ   Ⓔ

Answer: B

TIPS:

Make sure your student knows key concepts that come up in these types of questions, including geometric concepts such as rotational symmetry, line symmetry, parts of a whole.

If your student is finding these items difficult, encourage her to discover the pattern by looking in each direction (horizontally and vertically).
• Ask: "How do the objects change in the first row? Do you see a pattern? Do the objects change in the same way in the second row? The third row?"
• Ask: "How do the objects change in the first column? Do you see a pattern? Do the objects change in the same way in the second column? The third column?"

Encourage your student to isolate one element (e.g: outer shape, inner shape/s) and identify how it changes:
- Is the color/shading of the element changing as it moves?
- Is the element changing positions as it moves? Does it move up or down? Clockwise or counter-clockwise? Does it end up in the opposite (mirror) position?
- Does the element disappear and appear again as it move along the row/ column? Does it get bigger or smaller?

Encourage your student to make a prediction for the missing object and compare the description with the answer choices.

Serial Reasoning

With this question type, the student is shown a series of shapes that change across the rows and columns throughout the design. These questions require the student to understand how the objects in rows and columns relate to each other. The student must isolate and apply the rule/s in order to identify which object from the answer choices fits the empty box in the bottom right-hand corner of the matrix.

When your students encounters this kind of question for the first few times, say:

"Look at the picture. A piece is missing where you see the question mark. Show me the piece that is missing in the answer choices."

SAMPLE QUESTION:

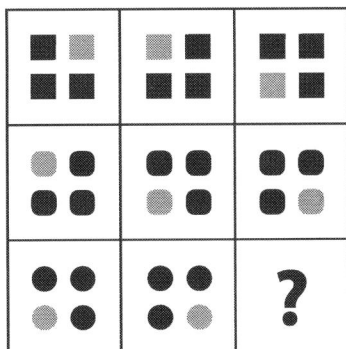

Ⓐ   Ⓑ   Ⓒ   Ⓓ   Ⓔ

Answer: B

TIPS:

Encourage your student to discover the pattern by looking in each direction.

• Ask: "How do the objects change in the first row (or first column)? Do you see a pattern? Do the objects change in the same way in the second row (or second column)? The third row (or third column)?"

• Diagonally (if the item is a 6-box matrix). Ask: "How do the objects change across the diagonal? Do you see a pattern?"

Encourage your student to isolate one element and identify how it changes.

• How does the color/shading of the element change as it moves along the row/column?

• Does the element change positions as it moves along the row/column? Does it move up, down or around (i.e.: clockwise, counter-clockwise). Does the element move to the opposite position?

• Does the element get bigger, smaller or stay the same as it moves? Does the element disappear and appear again as you move along the row/column?

Spatial Visualization

With this question type, a student is presented with a series of objects that combine, invert, transform and/or rotate across rows and columns. The student must identify the rule for the top row of objects and then predict what will happen to objects in the second (or third) row. Spatial Visualization items are widely seen to be the most difficult, particularly when involving objects that intersect in ways that are hard to recognize or involve an object rotating.

When your students encounters this kind of question for the first few times, say:

"A piece is missing where you see the question mark. Show me the missing piece in the answer choices."

SAMPLE QUESTION:

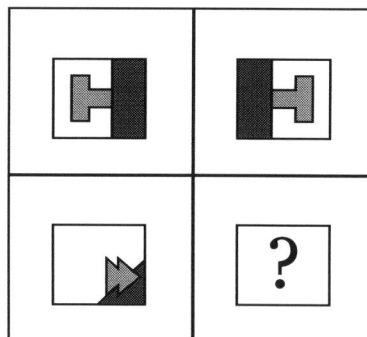

Answer: A

TIPS:

Ask your student to do some paper-folding projects. This will help her understand how objects on a folded piece of paper appear (and relate to each other) when the paper is opened.

Encourage your student to visualize -- observe, imagine and keep track of -- the changes in the geometric shapes as they move and then draw what she predicts she might see in the empty box.

Encourage your student to isolate one element (e.g: outer shape, inner shape/s) and identify how it changes.

- How does the color/shading of the element change as it moves along the row/column?
- Does the element change positions as it moves along the row/column?Does the element move to the opposite position?
- Does the element flip positions (e.g.: outer square becomes inner square or vice-versa)? Does the element go upside down?
- Does the element combine with another element?

NNAT® Level C
Practice Test Two

Answer bubble sheets can be found at the back of the book. Please make sure your student fills in each of the bubbles fully.

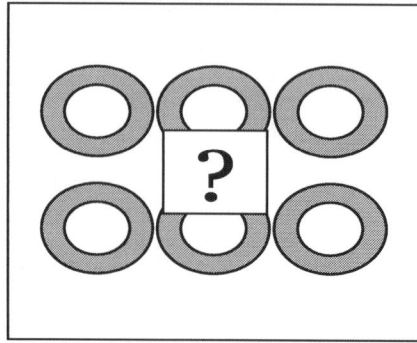

1

A B C D E

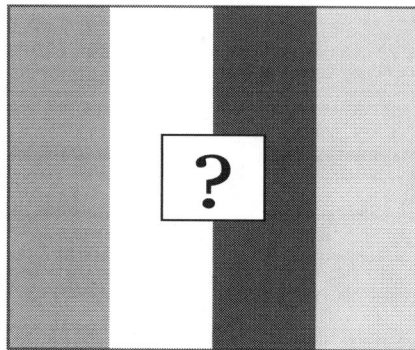

2

A B C D E

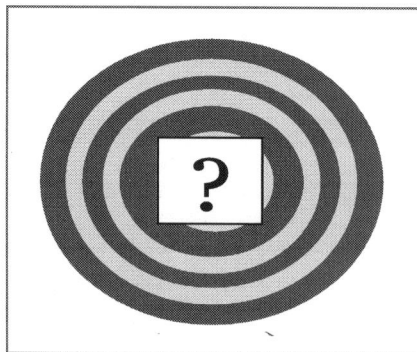

3

A B C D E

4

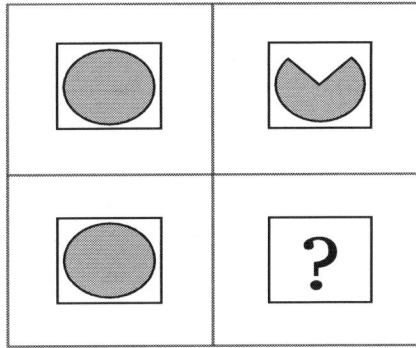

Ⓐ   Ⓑ   Ⓒ   Ⓓ   Ⓔ

5

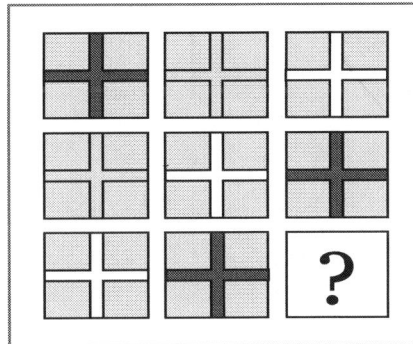

Ⓐ   Ⓑ   Ⓒ   Ⓓ   Ⓔ

6

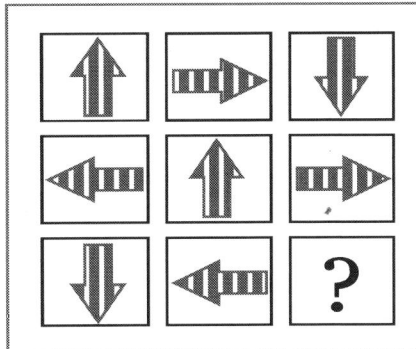

Ⓐ   Ⓑ   Ⓒ   Ⓓ   Ⓔ

7

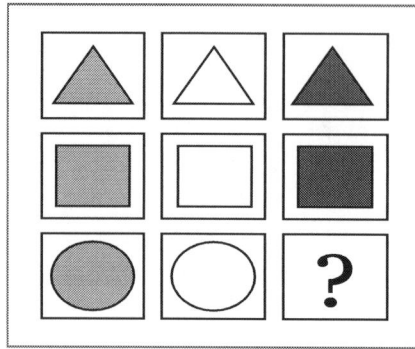

8

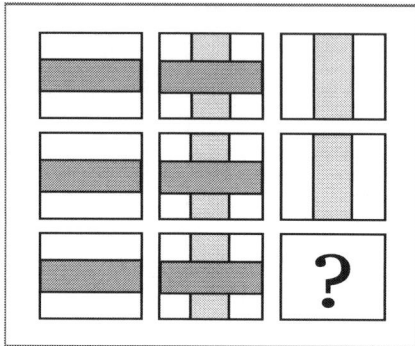

9

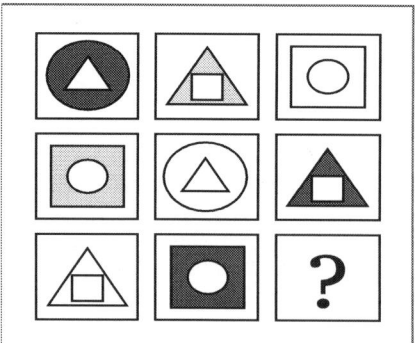

10

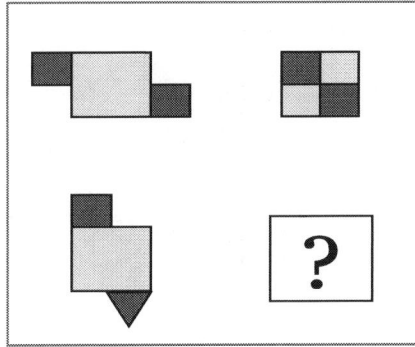

Ⓐ Ⓑ Ⓒ Ⓓ Ⓔ

11

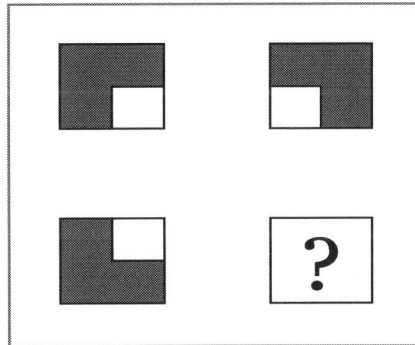

Ⓐ Ⓑ Ⓒ Ⓓ Ⓔ

12

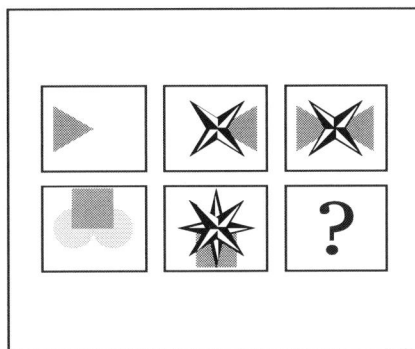

Ⓐ Ⓑ Ⓒ Ⓓ Ⓔ

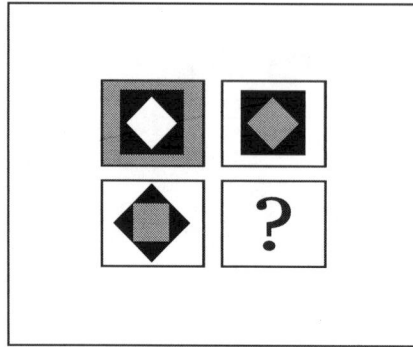

13

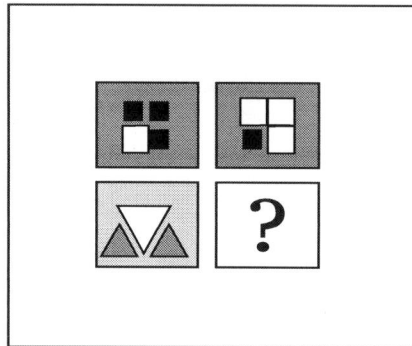

14

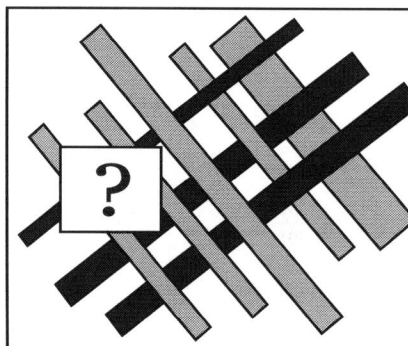

15

16

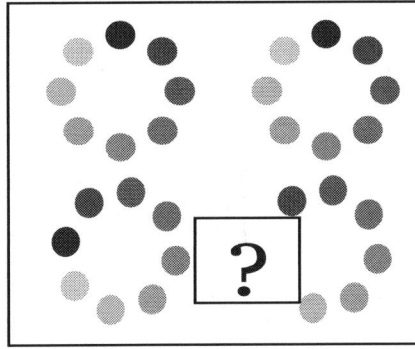

Ⓐ   Ⓑ   Ⓒ   Ⓓ   Ⓔ

17

Ⓐ   Ⓑ   Ⓒ   Ⓓ   Ⓔ

18

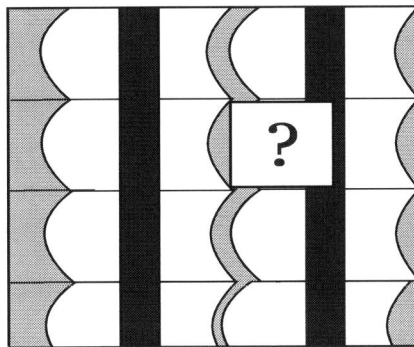

Ⓐ   Ⓑ   Ⓒ   Ⓓ   Ⓔ

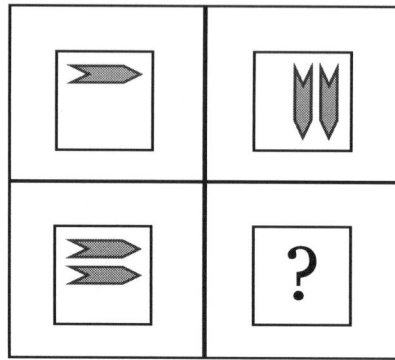

19

Ⓐ   Ⓑ   Ⓒ   Ⓓ   Ⓔ

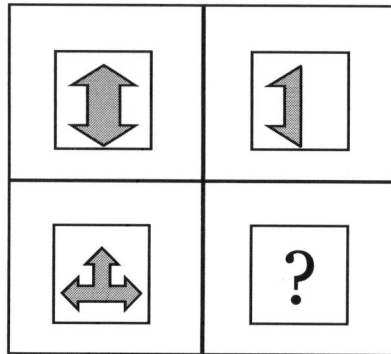

20

Ⓐ   Ⓑ   Ⓒ   Ⓓ   Ⓔ

21

Ⓐ   Ⓑ   Ⓒ   Ⓓ   Ⓔ

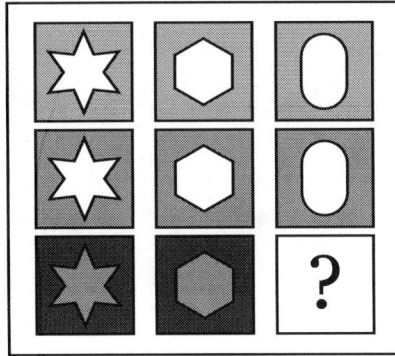

22

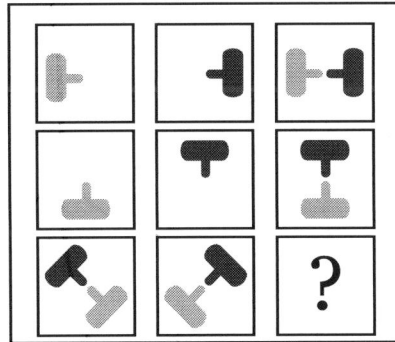

23

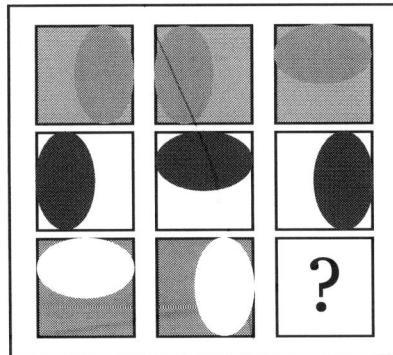

24

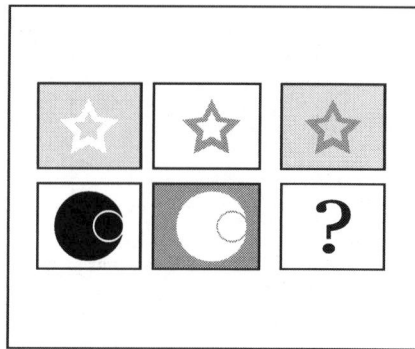

25

Ⓐ   Ⓑ   Ⓒ   Ⓓ   Ⓔ

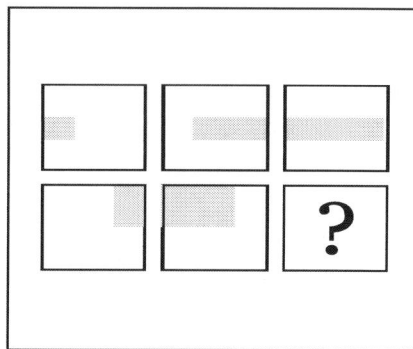

26

Ⓐ   Ⓑ   Ⓒ   Ⓓ   Ⓔ

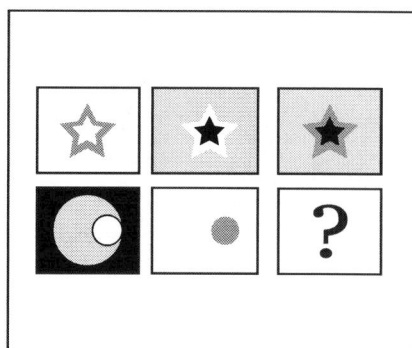

27

Ⓐ   Ⓑ   Ⓒ   Ⓓ   Ⓔ

28

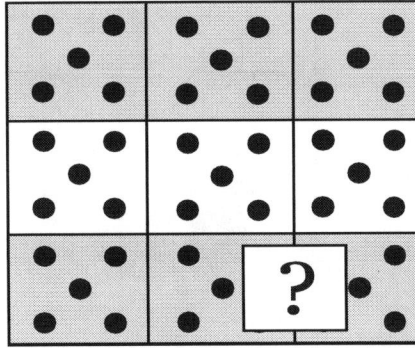

Ⓐ   Ⓑ   Ⓒ   Ⓓ   Ⓔ

29

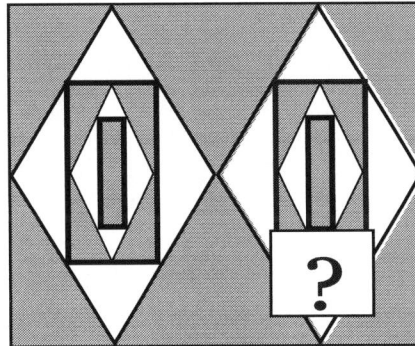

Ⓐ   Ⓑ   Ⓒ   Ⓓ   Ⓔ

30

Ⓐ   Ⓑ   Ⓒ   Ⓓ   Ⓔ

31

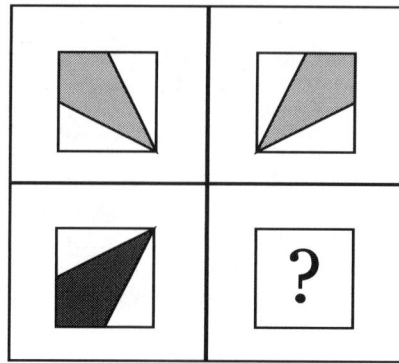

Ⓐ Ⓑ Ⓒ Ⓓ Ⓔ

32

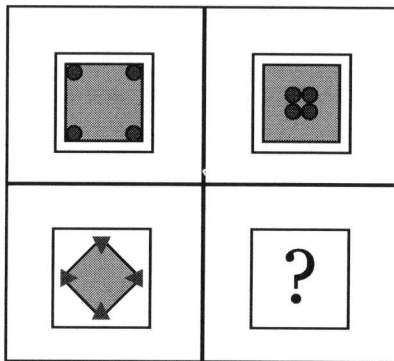

Ⓐ Ⓑ Ⓒ Ⓓ Ⓔ

33

Ⓐ Ⓑ Ⓒ Ⓓ Ⓔ

34

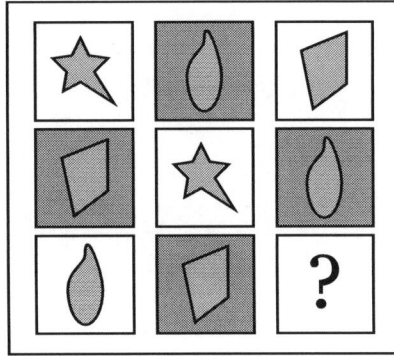

Ⓐ   Ⓑ   Ⓒ   Ⓓ   Ⓔ

35

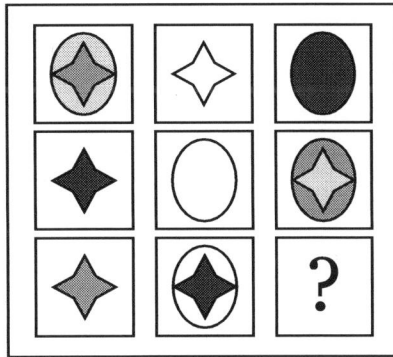

Ⓐ   Ⓑ   Ⓒ   Ⓓ   Ⓔ

36

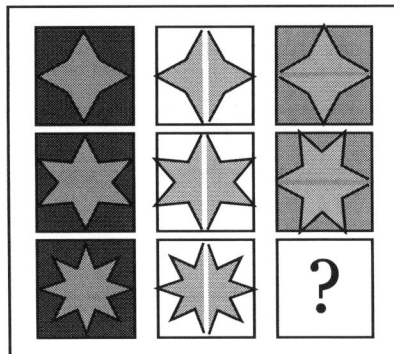

Ⓐ   Ⓑ   Ⓒ   Ⓓ   Ⓔ

37

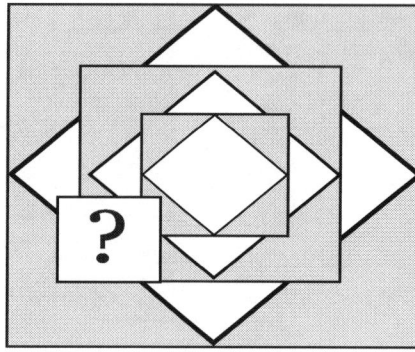

Ⓐ   Ⓑ   Ⓒ   Ⓓ   Ⓔ

38

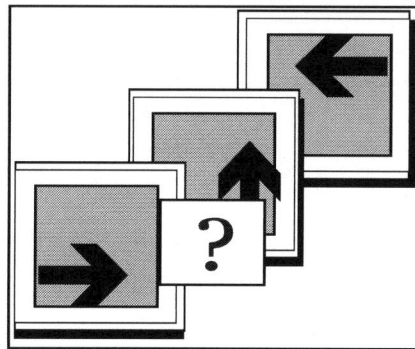

Ⓐ   Ⓑ   Ⓒ   Ⓓ   Ⓔ

39

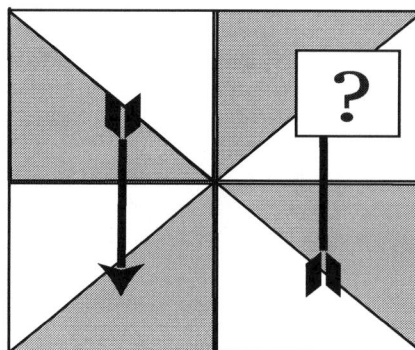

Ⓐ   Ⓑ   Ⓒ   Ⓓ   Ⓔ

40

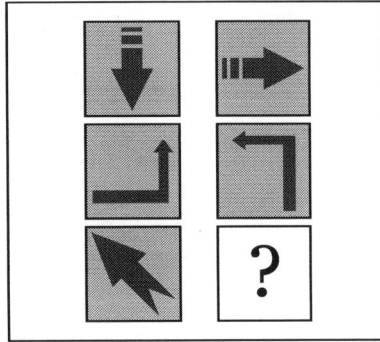

(A)   (B)   (C)   (D)   (E)

41

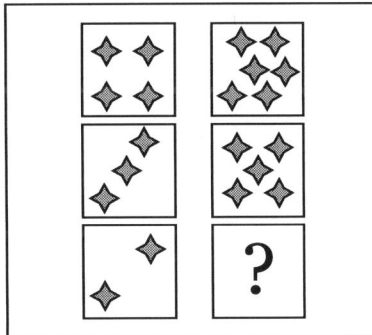

(A)   (B)   (C)   (D)   (E)

42

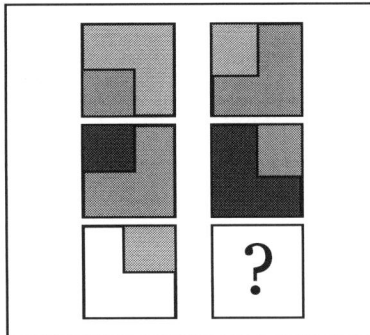

(A)   (B)   (C)   (D)   (E)

43

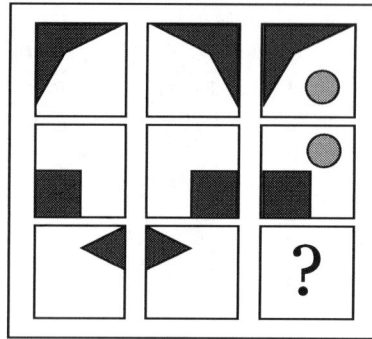

Ⓐ   Ⓑ   Ⓒ   Ⓓ   Ⓔ

44

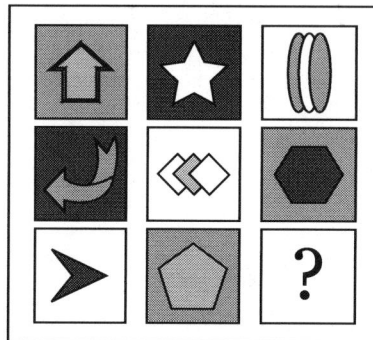

Ⓐ   Ⓑ   Ⓒ   Ⓓ   Ⓔ

45

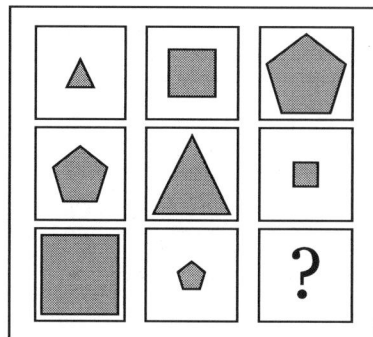

Ⓐ   Ⓑ   Ⓒ   Ⓓ   Ⓔ

46

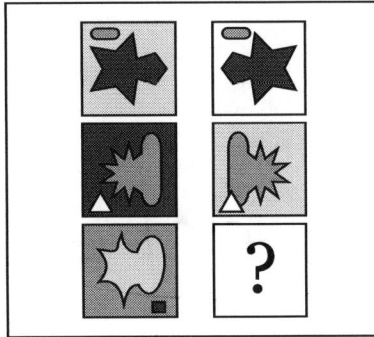

Ⓐ   Ⓑ   Ⓒ   Ⓓ   Ⓔ

47

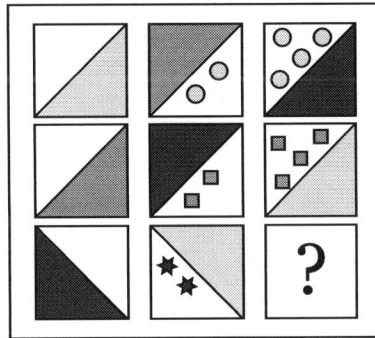

Ⓐ   Ⓑ   Ⓒ   Ⓓ   Ⓔ

48

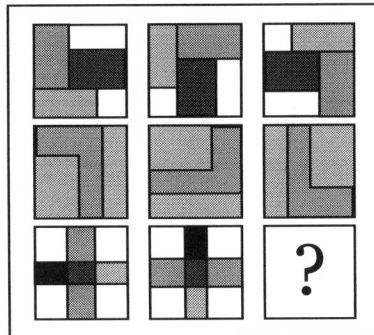

Ⓐ   Ⓑ   Ⓒ   Ⓓ   Ⓔ

NNAT® Level C
Bubble Sheet
& Answers

Practice Test

Use a No. 2 Pencil
Fill in bubble completely.

Ⓐ ● Ⓒ Ⓓ

Name:_____   Date:_____

1. Ⓐ Ⓑ Ⓒ Ⓓ Ⓔ   26. Ⓐ Ⓑ Ⓒ Ⓓ Ⓔ

2. Ⓐ Ⓑ Ⓒ Ⓓ Ⓔ   27. Ⓐ Ⓑ Ⓒ Ⓓ Ⓔ

3. Ⓐ Ⓑ Ⓒ Ⓓ Ⓔ   28. Ⓐ Ⓑ Ⓒ Ⓓ Ⓔ

4. Ⓐ Ⓑ Ⓒ Ⓓ Ⓔ   29. Ⓐ Ⓑ Ⓒ Ⓓ Ⓔ

5. Ⓐ Ⓑ Ⓒ Ⓓ Ⓔ   30. Ⓐ Ⓑ Ⓒ Ⓓ Ⓔ

6. Ⓐ Ⓑ Ⓒ Ⓓ Ⓔ   31. Ⓐ Ⓑ Ⓒ Ⓓ Ⓔ

7. Ⓐ Ⓑ Ⓒ Ⓓ Ⓔ   32. Ⓐ Ⓑ Ⓒ Ⓓ Ⓔ

8. Ⓐ Ⓑ Ⓒ Ⓓ Ⓔ   33. Ⓐ Ⓑ Ⓒ Ⓓ Ⓔ

9. Ⓐ Ⓑ Ⓒ Ⓓ Ⓔ   34. Ⓐ Ⓑ Ⓒ Ⓓ Ⓔ

10. Ⓐ Ⓑ Ⓒ Ⓓ Ⓔ   35. Ⓐ Ⓑ Ⓒ Ⓓ Ⓔ

11. Ⓐ Ⓑ Ⓒ Ⓓ Ⓔ   36. Ⓐ Ⓑ Ⓒ Ⓓ Ⓔ

12. Ⓐ Ⓑ Ⓒ Ⓓ Ⓔ   37. Ⓐ Ⓑ Ⓒ Ⓓ Ⓔ

13. Ⓐ Ⓑ Ⓒ Ⓓ Ⓔ   38. Ⓐ Ⓑ Ⓒ Ⓓ Ⓔ

14. Ⓐ Ⓑ Ⓒ Ⓓ Ⓔ   39. Ⓐ Ⓑ Ⓒ Ⓓ Ⓔ

15. Ⓐ Ⓑ Ⓒ Ⓓ Ⓔ   40. Ⓐ Ⓑ Ⓒ Ⓓ Ⓔ

16. Ⓐ Ⓑ Ⓒ Ⓓ Ⓔ   41. Ⓐ Ⓑ Ⓒ Ⓓ Ⓔ

17. Ⓐ Ⓑ Ⓒ Ⓓ Ⓔ   42. Ⓐ Ⓑ Ⓒ Ⓓ Ⓔ

18. Ⓐ Ⓑ Ⓒ Ⓓ Ⓔ   43. Ⓐ Ⓑ Ⓒ Ⓓ Ⓔ

19. Ⓐ Ⓑ Ⓒ Ⓓ Ⓔ   44. Ⓐ Ⓑ Ⓒ Ⓓ Ⓔ

20. Ⓐ Ⓑ Ⓒ Ⓓ Ⓔ   45. Ⓐ Ⓑ Ⓒ Ⓓ Ⓔ

21. Ⓐ Ⓑ Ⓒ Ⓓ Ⓔ   46. Ⓐ Ⓑ Ⓒ Ⓓ Ⓔ

22. Ⓐ Ⓑ Ⓒ Ⓓ Ⓔ   47. Ⓐ Ⓑ Ⓒ Ⓓ Ⓔ

23. Ⓐ Ⓑ Ⓒ Ⓓ Ⓔ   48. Ⓐ Ⓑ Ⓒ Ⓓ Ⓔ

24. Ⓐ Ⓑ Ⓒ Ⓓ Ⓔ

25. Ⓐ Ⓑ Ⓒ Ⓓ Ⓔ

Answer Explanations

Please note that there are often various ways to solve the puzzles. These answer explantions provide one option for solving each puzzle. The answer explanations provide the correct answer for both the 'color' and 'black and white' versions of the book (the black/white/ gray shade are referenced, when relevant, in brackets).

Download a color version of this book at:
https://originstutoring.lpages.co/nnat135

1. **E.** The puzzle piece completes the pattern.

2. **D.** The puzzle piece completes the pattern.

3. **A.** The puzzle piece completes the pattern.

4. **C.** From left to right, the shape in the top row changes from a circle to a circle with a segment removed. The color of the items remains the same across the row.

5. **D.** The background color stays the same across the rows, but the color of the flag alternates.

6. **B.** Moving from the left to right box, the striped arrow is rotated 90 degrees clockwise, and the stripes change direction.

7. **E.** The background color and the shape stay the same across the rows, but the shape's color/shade alternates.

8. **A.** The shape retains the same color and orientation down the column.

9. **C.** The inner white shapes alternate across the rows and down the columns, while the larger outer figure alternates shape and color across the rows and columns.

10. **A.** The dark color/shade flaps fold inward to create the right hand pattern.

11. **B.** The item is flipped across the vertical axis.

12. **D.** Across the row, the items stack/combine, forming the pattern in the third column.

13. **A.** The colors alternate from innermost to outermost object. Or, the puzzle can be solved by seeing that (moving from left to right) white becomes green (gray), black remains black, and green (gray) becomes white.

14. **B.** Moving from left to right, the inner figures change size and color. The background remains the same color.

15. **D.** The puzzle piece completes the pattern.

16. **E.** The puzzle piece completes the pattern.

17. **D.** The puzzle piece completes the pattern.

18. **C.** The puzzle piece completes the pattern.

19. **B.** Moving from the left to right box, another arrow of the same color is added and both the arrows are rotated 90 degrees clockwise.

20. **E.** Moving from the left to right box, the left half of the arrow shapes are displayed.

21. **C.** The shape in the bottom left box is the mirror image (flipped vertically) of the shape in the top left box. Also the shading is reversed.

22. **D.** Boxes in each row have the same color background, but the shape alternates between a star, a hexagon and an oval. The boxes in each column contain the same shape.

23. **B.** Moving from left to right box, the shapes in the boxes combine to form the shape in the third column. The color of each shape is retained.

24. **A.** Across each row and down each column, an ellipse is touching the left, right and top edges of the three boxes.

25. **D.** The shapes overlap to form the final pattern in the third column.

26. B. The shapes combine to form the new shape in the third column.

27. E. The shapes overlap to form the final pattern in the third column.

28. A. The puzzle piece completes the pattern.

29. E. The puzzle piece completes the pattern.

30. D. The puzzle piece completes the pattern.

31. A. Moving from the left to right box, the shape is flipped horizontally and the color is retained.

32. D. Moving from the left to right box, the circles at the corners unite to form a shape in the middle and the color is retained.

33. E. Moving from the left to right box, the stars interchange their position and colors.

34. E. Each row alternates between 3 shapes. Each column also alternates between the 3 same shapes. Adjacent boxes alternate background color/shade.

35. C. Each row alternates between a star, an ellipse and a combination of the two shapes. In each row, the colors/shades of the shape/s in each box alternate. In the bottom row, the oval is the shape missing, and light gray (light blue) is the missing color.

36. A. Moving from the left to right, the star is divided into two equal halves across the vertical and then the horizontal axis. The color of the background alternates across the rows. The color of the star and the background stays the same in each column.

37. C. The puzzle piece completes the pattern.

38. E. The puzzle piece completes the pattern.

39. B. The puzzle piece completes the pattern.

40. B. Moving from the left to right, the arrow is rotated 90 counterclockwise and the color is retained.

41. A. Moving from the left to right box, two more stars are added and the color is retained.

42. C. Moving from the left to right box, the shape is rotated 90 degrees clockwise and the colors are swapped.

43. D. Moving from the left to middle box, the shape is horizontally flipped. Moving from the middle to right box, the shape is again horizontally flipped (so it is the same as the shape in the left frame) and a colored circle is added.

44. E. Each frame has shapes that do not repeat. Therefore the answer choices C and E can be considered. Also a row is composed of three frames with alternate color backgrounds. The bottom right frame must have a dark gray (dark blue) background.

45. C. Each row has a triangle, a square and a pentagon – one small, another medium sized and another large. In the bottom row, a large square and a small pentagon are present. Therefore the bottom right box must have a medium sized triangle.

46. E. Moving from the left to right, the complex shape is flipped horizontally while the smaller shape is left undisturbed at the same position. Although the color of the two shapes is retained, the color of the background changes.

47. C. Moving from the left to right, the triangle shape is flipped 180 degrees across the diagonal and alternates color. In the middle boxes, two smaller shapes of the same color/shade (as the first triangle in left boxes) are added. Moving from the middle to right boxes, three additional smaller shapes of the same color are added (to create five small shapes) while they move to the opposite half of the box.

48. A. Moving from the left to right, the shape is rotated 90 clockwise.

DOWNLOAD THE PRACTICE TEST
IN COLOR

If you also want the COLOR version of this book, please go to the following link to download it!

Please visit
https://originstutoring.lpages.co/nnat135
to access a color version of your practice test.

Thank you for selecting this book. We would be thrilled if you left us a review on the website where you bought this book!

Made in the USA
Las Vegas, NV
22 August 2023